GROW YOUR OWN!

The best way to read this book is to begin at the beginning and read all the way through. You'll be amazed at what you'll find out. But if you want to read about one particular thing, such as mung beans or eelworms, look in the index on page 33.

Thompson Yardley wrote this book and drew the pictures. He has done a lot of other things as well as writing books, such as repairing boilers and delivering milk.

British Library C.I.P.
Yardley, Thompson,
Grow Your Own! (Spaceship Earth)
1. Organic gardening – vegetables (junior)
1. Title II. Series.
635.0484

ISBN   0 304 32539 2 (hardback)
       0 304 32691 7 (paperback)

First published in 1992 by
Cassell Publishers Limited
Villiers House, 41/47 Strand
London WC2N 5JE

Printed and bound in Hong Kong by
Dah Hua Printing Press Co. Ltd.

WHERE DO **VEGETABLES** COME FROM?

THE VEG RACK!

THE FREEZER!

But before that?..

But before that?..

FRUIT AND VEGETABLES

THE SHOPS!

A FARM!

Giles' "FARM FRESH" VEGETABLE PRODUCE

But **where** on a farm?

THE SOIL!

PROD!

Yes! Isn't it amazing? All of our vegetables come from lovely, grubby soil. You can be a vegetable farmer too.

FIND OUT ABOUT...
· Healthy soil!
· Friendly pests!
· Helpful weeds!
· Dibbers!

DIBBERS??

1

SOIL

SOIL looks like dead muck. But in fact it's teeming with tiny creatures and growths. Imagine you're very tiny too. Here's what it might be like to explore the soil!..

Plant leaves breathe air. Plants also need sunlight which gives them the energy to grow.

The top part of the soil usually has lots of humus in it. Humus is the remains of dead plants, dead animals and animal droppings.

The humus is mixed up with bits of clay and sand. These contain particles of chemicals such as iron, silicon and potassium. Plants feed on these chemicals.

Humus is spongy and stops rainwater from soaking away.

SLURRP!!

Plant roots take up the water and soil chemicals so that the plant above can grow.

Run! It's a grub!

No! It's an eelworm! We're ITS grub!

Yummy! Grub!

Lots of tiny animals such as grubs, worms and eelworms live in soil too. They feed on humus, roots and each other!

BIG WORM FACT

The world's largest worm lives in Australia. It grows up to a metre long!

G'day!

Gasp!

Watch out for fungi!

Thin strands of fungi spread through soil. Fungi need food and water, just like plants, but they don't need sunlight. Most fungi break down dead matter and turn it into useful soil chemicals for plants to feed on.

EEK!

Phew!

SNATCH!

Some fungi feed on living things. One type of fungus feeds on eelworms. It forms itself into sticky loops to trap its food!

NIBBLE!

CHOMP!

And there are billions of bacteria in a lump of soil. They mostly feed on dead vegetation. Their waste products contain nitrogen which plants need.

Nice plant!

Nice bacteria!

Some bacteria live in clumps on pea, bean and clover plant roots. These plants produce food for the bacteria. The bacteria produce nitrogen from the air for the plants. They get on very well!

MUNCH!

We rely on the soil to grow plants for farm animals to eat too.

TROMP!

And we rely on farmers to look after the soil so we have plenty of plants to eat!

In 1846 there were a billion people in the world. By the year 2000 there will be six billion. This population explosion is the world's most important problem. We need more and more food each year. And more and more land to farm.

HOMELESS ANIMALS

Unfortunately, modern

FARMING

methods cause lots of

PROBLEMS!..

LAND AND WILDLIFE DAMAGE

Some rain forests in poor countries are being cut down to make room for crops and cattle. But rain forest soil isn't good enough for farming. Its small supply of soil chemicals becomes quickly used up. Deserts form. And wildlife dies when its forest homes are cut down.

PESTS AND DISEASES

In rich countries, massive fields of crops are grown. This gives huge numbers of pests and diseases the chance to attack their favourite foods. And growing the same crops all the time weakens the soil. Weak soil produces weak plants.

NIBBLE!

GNASH!

RASP!

SOIL POISONING

So farmers use poisonous pesticides to kill the pests. And they add artificial fertilizers to force their crops to grow. BUT... pesticides also kill harmless or useful wildlife, such as bees. And artificial fertilizers damage the soil, so that worms and helpful bacteria can't grow. Pesticides and fertilizers may also get into our food!

ZZUB!

PESTO

Eurgh!

LOSS OF CHOICE

There are about ten thousand different edible plants. How many can you name? And there are lots of varieties of each crop. For example, how many types of apple can you name? Farmers find it easier to grow just a few types of plants. So you can usually only buy one type of each plant in the shops. People need to eat a wide variety of food to stay healthy.

What sorts of vegetables do you have?

Cabbages!

Cabbagey sort of cabbages!

What sort of cabbages are they?

O.K. I'll have one!

HIGH COSTS

Modern farmers buy lots of seeds, pesticides, fertilizers and farm machinery. The crops have to be transported, stored and tidied up to look pretty in the shops. All this costs money. You pay for all these things when you buy the vegetables.

How much is it?

Fifty pounds please!

I'm feeling proper poorly today, doctor!

You must have been out of your bed too long, Mr. Carrot!

STALE FOOD

Vegetables contain vitamins and other chemicals. We need these chemicals so as to stay healthy. BUT... vegetables start to lose their vitamins as soon as they're harvested. It may take days or weeks to get farm vegetables to your table. And canned vegetables sometimes have no vitamins at all!

Phew! I'm glad those two pages are over!

Yeah! It was horrible!

Huh! It wasn't that bad! (phew!)

Some farmers are damaging the soil by poisoning or overusing it. But we will need to get more and more out of the soil to feed our growing population.

What will we do in the future?..

Fortunately, there are some farmers who look after the soil. They don't use artificial soil chemicals. They're called organic farmers. And all the farming problems on pages six and seven have...

PHEW!

ORGANIC ANSWERS!

If you've got a small patch of soil to use, you could be an organic farmer too!..

~ BEETLE TOWERS ~
BED AND BREAKFAST

COMFY MULCH BED

~BREAKFAST~
FRUIT
MAGGOTS!

CONSERVATION

There's not much room for wild plants, animals and insects on modern farms. You could help them by making habitats in town. And you'll find that they'll help you in return!

There's a nice little cabbage field!

Let's lay our eggs there!

No! There's more caterpillar food in this BIG cabbage field!

O.K.

SMALL FIELDS

Small fields are good. They stop huge numbers of pests from building up. And rotating crops from year to year helps to keep the soil fertile and disease-free.

Dinnertime Willy!

THRRRP!

NIB!
NIB!
NIB!

SOIL CARE

Organic farmers and gardeners try to make sure that their soil is healthy. They use compost and organic manures. These encourage helpful bacteria and earthworms to do their work.

Worms eat dead leaves. And their wastes feed the soil!

SOME UNUSUAL APPLES...

Beauty of Bath

Golden Hornet

Egremont Russet

Peasgood Nonsuch

CROP VARIETY

Do you get bored eating the same old fruit and veg? So do organic farmers. They like to grow unusual and old-fashioned varieties of plants. How many sorts of apples did you name? (page 7).
Have you heard of these?

LOCAL FARMING

Imagine you've got vegetables in your garden. You'd only need to pop out of your back door to get your food. This saves the cost of transport and storage. If you grow vegetables indoors you needn't even leave the table!

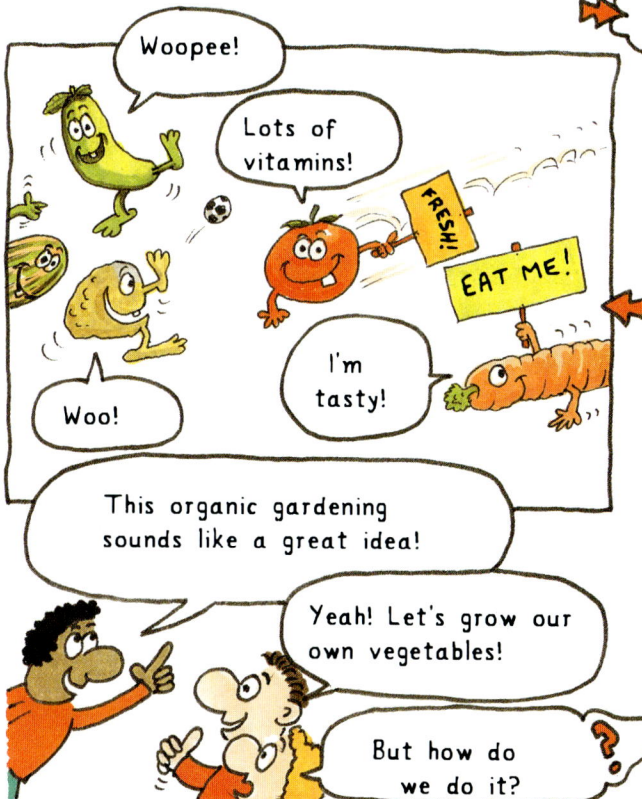

Mmm! Fresh tomatoes!

Mmm! Fresh beans!

Mmm! Fresh cucumbers!

EEK!

FRESH FOOD

Top cooks always buy fresh vegetables. They taste better than ones which are days or weeks old. And vegetables straight from the soil are full of vitamins.

Woopee!

Lots of vitamins!

FRESH!

EAT ME!

I'm tasty!

Woo!

This organic gardening sounds like a great idea!

Yeah! Let's grow our own vegetables!

But how do we do it?

It's easy to be an organic farmer. The hardest part is finding out how to start!..

You'll need to do a few things before you

GET STARTED!..

1. GET A PLOT

No, not that sort of plot!

A vegetable plot is a patch of ground where vegetables are grown. Is there an unused plot in your garden? Or in a friend's garden? Don't worry if you can't get a plot. Why not ask one of your teachers if you can set up a small farm at your school?

2. GET A NOTEBOOK...

... and get used to writing in it! It's easy to forget where you've planted your crops...

Use the book for all your farming notes.

3. DRAW A ROUGH PLAN

of your garden. Measure your plot. For your first year of crops don't take on too much. Between 2 and 6 square metres of soil is plenty. Draw a bigger plan of your plot when you've decided what to grow.

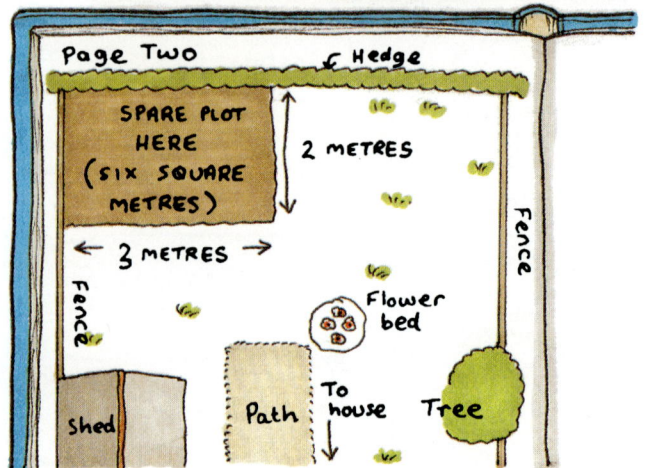

4. FIND OUT ABOUT YOUR PLOT

All plants have to have the right conditions to grow. For instance, carrots won't grow in a desert. And bananas won't grow at the North Pole! SO...

- What type of soil is your plot?
- Is it well drained?
- How much shelter is there?
- What's your local climate like?
- Which crops will grow best?

How do we find out all that?

I dunno!

Huh! Let's give up!

This might sound a lot to find out. But help is at hand! You could find out about your plot from...

- Parents
- Your teacher
- Gardening neighbours

Most gardeners will talk for hours about plants!

And then there's beetroots. I remember one year when... blah blah... and you've got to watch out for gribble flies... blah... bore bore... acid or alkaline... blah blah yak... chalk... talk... ... rabbit... bull... blah...

~YAWNS~

And here's your best friend, the earthworm. Say hello, Willy!

I'm shy!

And you can find out if there's an organic farm near where you live. If there is, ask your parents or teacher to take you for a visit.
Organic farmers know a lot about soil and soil creatures...

Remember to write down everything you find out.

Of course, one important place you should visit is your local garden centre...

11

You can ask for advice at

THE GARDEN CENTRE...

Get one of your parents to take you. Some garden centres are organic, and others aren't. In any case, they'll know which plants will grow in your neighbourhood. Remember to write down what you find out. And don't buy too much. Remember you've only got a small plot!

WHAT YOU NEED...

A BAG OF ORGANIC COMPOST

Compost is the nearly dry, rotted remains of dead plants. You'll need to dig some of this into your soil. It helps to feed helpful bacteria and plant roots. And it helps to keep soil moist and crumbly.

A SPRAYER

You'll find a cheap, hand-operated sprayer useful later on in the year.

MARKERS

(And a permanent ink pen).

GLOVES

Some people have sensitive skin. It's a good idea to wear gardening gloves when handling soil.

WHAT YOU DON'T NEED...

PEAT

Peat also helps to improve soil. But it's dug from moorlands and bogs where animals and plants live. They lose their homes when the peat they live on is dug from under them.

CHEMICALS

Remember – you're an organic farmer now. That means artificial pesticides and fertilizers are right out!

Most of the items in garden centres are useful. But they cost a lot! So if you havn't got a lot to spend...

DON'T BUY MUCH!

You can make most of the gardening items you need by
RECYCLING OTHER THINGS...

SEED TRAYS

You can use old paint trays or pizza trays. Get an adult to jab a few small holes in the bottom. Put pebbles in the bottom and fill up with soil before planting your seeds.

MARKERS

Cut squeezy bottles into strips.

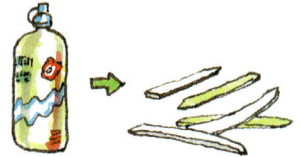

CLOCHES

Cloches help to protect small plants. Make your cloches from plastic drinks bottles. Take off the label. Cut off the bottom. Push into the soil.

PLANT POTS

Use margarine tubs, yoghurt pots or big plastic paint pots. Clean them out. Drill one large hole in the bottom of each.

SUPPORTS

If you grow beans, you'll need sticks for them to climb up. You can use any strong, thin sticks about 1 metre long.

A DIBBER

This is for making holes in the soil for seeds. Use a bit of old broomstick or the handle of a broken spade.

DIB! DIB!

OTHER TOOLS

You should be able to borrow larger tools from a neighbour. Write down who you borrowed them from!

Spade
Rake
Trowel
Big watering can

One thing you'll definitely need to buy is

SEEDS...

WHAT TO GROW?...

Only buy enough seeds to match the size of your patch. Plant no more than about six easy-to-grow vegetables. By next year you'll know a lot more. Then you can try other vegetables. Some seeds won't sprout. And some of your plants may die. But... DON'T PANIC!

Here are six vegetables which most people will find easy to grow...

FAST FIRST FRUIT FACT

You can buy special fruit seeds which will grow into plants very quickly. But you won't get any fruit from them for two or more years. And fruit-growing is much harder than growing vegetables.

Are you going to grow, or what?

No!

Why not?

My feet are cold!

LITTLE PLUM

Most vegetables grow and produce food after a few months. Stick to growing vegetables until you know a bit more about farming.

1. BROCCOLI

Purple broccoli   Calabrese broccoli

Broccoli is part of the cabbage family. There are several types. Purple broccoli is the easiest to grow. Plant in spring, harvest in late autumn.

2. COURGETTES

Courgettes are young marrows. They like a lot of compost. Pick them off the plants when each grows to about 8 cm long. This encourages other courgettes to form and take their place.

3. RADISHES

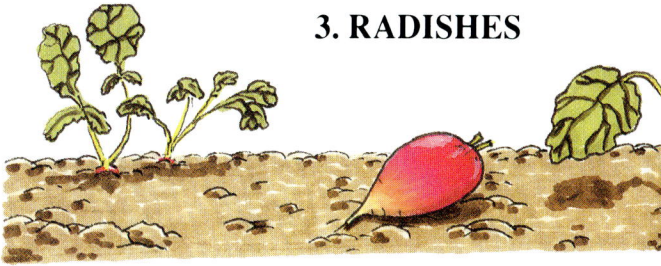

Believe it or not, this is another member of the cabbage family! Easy to grow. They grow quickly and may be ready to harvest all at the same time. You can buy packets of "salad mixed" radishes. These are all slightly different sorts which are ready to pick at different times.

4. RUNNER BEANS

These need sticks to climb up. Sow them when there's no danger of frost. You can pick the beans off the plants as they become ready. Keep them watered regularly. Beans help to keep aphids away from cabbage-like plants.

5. SUNFLOWERS

You can grow these almost anywhere. They may grow up to 2 metres tall! You can't eat the plants, but you can eat the seeds. Pick them off, dry them and shell them first. Birds love them too, so you've got to be quick!

6. TURNIPS

Another member of the cabbage family. Don't plant them all at once or you may end up with too many to eat! Plant a batch every three weeks from late spring to late autumn. Harvest them as they become ready.

Read everything on each seed packet. Try to match what you know about your plot to what each vegetable needs. If you're farming a plot with friends, make sure you all agree on what to grow!..

I want sunflowers!

No! Let's have asparagus!

What about "Burpless Tasty Green Cucumbers"? They sound silly!

Let's vote!

15

WHAT THE PACKET SAYS...

There are always lots of instructions on seed packets. But sometimes you have to be an expert to understand the instructions!
Gardeners use special gardening words and phrases. Here are some you may come across...

"Germination"? We don't want any germs!

SQUEEZE!

"Thin out" the seedlings?.. What??

GERMINATION

This is another word for sprouting. When the soil, the weather and the time of year are right, a seed in soil will sprout. First it splits open. Then a white shoot grows up. Then tiny leaves show on the surface of the soil.

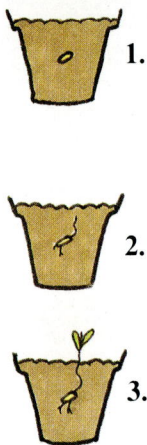

1.

2.

3.

HARDENING OFF

1.

2.

3.

Some plants won't grow in cold soil. These need to be grown indoors in pots or trays first. When the weather has warmed up, these pots are put outdoors. When the soil has warmed up, the seedlings can be replanted in the soil.

MULCHING

Bare soil can be kept moist or warm by putting something over it. This covering can be bark chips, plastic sheets, old carpet – almost anything!

Old carpet strips

1. Bunched up seedlings...

2. Properly spaced out seedlings...

THINNING OUT

When you're sowing small seeds, it's hard to keep them in separate holes. The plants may grow up in bunches. If they do, they won't grow very well. The weaker-looking plants have to be pulled up. This gives the healthy ones a chance to grow properly.

16

You can't really GROW plants. They do this by themselves! But you can encourage them to grow. Planting is the first important thing to do. Here's...

HOW TO PLANT PLANTS...

1. Clear away any odds and ends lying about on your plot.

Ay? What?

HEAVE!

2. Get an adult to show you how to dig. Shovel in some compost as it's done. A 'LARGE' size bag is enough for 10 square metres.

Gasp!

Watch that worm!

3. Rake the soil flat so it's smooth but crumbly. Don't tread on it. Plants like damp crumbly soil.

4. Water the soil well. Let it soak in for a few hours.

Don't tread on the soil!

5. Dib rows of holes for large seeds. Drop in seeds and cover.

DIB! DIB!

6. Use the rake's edge to make shallow grooves for small seeds. Sprinkle in the seeds and cover.

7. Put in plastic markers. Jot everything down in your notebook.

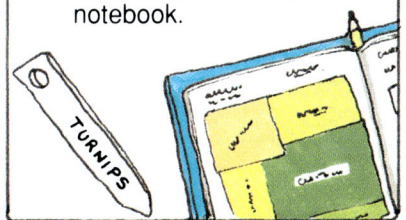

TURNIPS

8. Some vegetable seedlings need to be hardened off. You can do this by starting them off on a warm window sill. Then put them near the back door later. Keep the soil moist but not too wet.

9. After all that hard work, you deserve a nice cup of tea!

SLURP!

HAH!

Wow! We're gardeners

DRIBBLE!

Here are three creatures which live in the soil. When they've eaten and grown enough, they turn into adults. The adults look completely different, and live above the soil.

Can you solve the

SOIL PUZZLE?

Which one of these three soil creatures will live long enough to turn into an adult?..

WIREWORM

CUTWORM

LEATHER-JACKET

Eat some plant stems

Eat some plant roots

Watch out for that carrot bait. Oh, no! You've just been trapped by an organic gardener!

EEK! Sorry!

Eat some grass roots

Eat some carrot roots

You got too near the surface. Too bad! You've just been eaten by a blackbird!

PECK!

Eat some plant roots

The cutworm would have turned into a moth.

Answer:

The wireworm would have turned into a beetle.

The leather-jacket will turn into a daddy longlegs.

While you've been doing that puzzle, have the birds been eating your seeds? Some birds are good for your garden. But crows or pigeons may eat your seeds and seedlings. Then you won't get any plants! You could get an adult to help you to...

MAKE A SCARECROW!

1. Nail two pieces of wood together. Make a cross shape about as long as a tall person.

2. Fill plastic bags with paper. Tie them to the cross.

3. Dress the scarecrow with old clothes. Buy or make an ugly mask too. Leave the clothes loose and flappy.

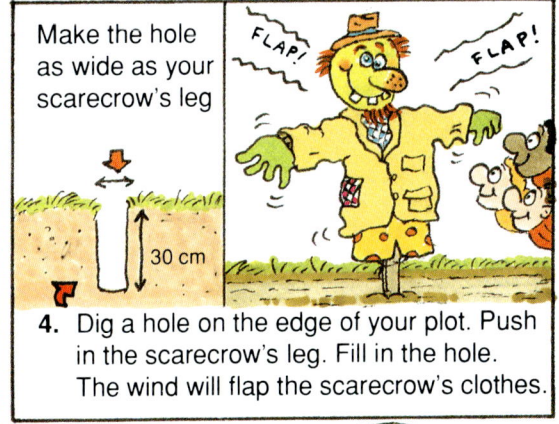

Make the hole as wide as your scarecrow's leg

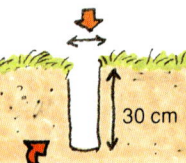

30 cm

4. Dig a hole on the edge of your plot. Push in the scarecrow's leg. Fill in the hole. The wind will flap the scarecrow's clothes.

Some birds aren't scared of scarecrows. Here's another way to protect your plants...

1. Bang in a few sticks around your plot.

2. Tie some white string between the sticks.

3. Tie on rattly things like tin lids, ring pulls or bits of plastic. Birds don't like noisy, flappy things.

Eek!

RATTLE!

Some small animals aren't put off by string or scarecrows. Animals which try to eat your food are usually called pests. But no pests are completely bad. It's better to think of them as

UNWELCOME GUESTS!

Some of them eat your plants. Others may accidentally spread fungus diseases. Watch out for these unwelcome pest-guests on your crops...

APHIDS

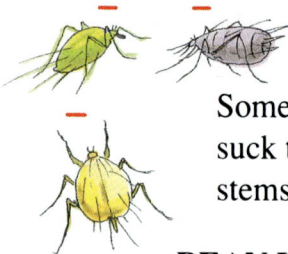

These are also called greenfly and blackfly. Some are even yellow! They suck the sap from the leaves and stems of most plants.

BEAN WEEVILS

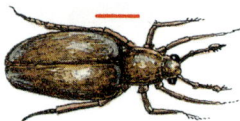

These feed on pea and bean leaves.

CATERPILLARS

Large White butterfly caterpillar

Small White butterfly caterpillar

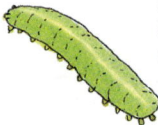

Eggs

Several types of butterfly lay eggs on cabbage family plants. The eggs hatch into caterpillars which eat the leaves. The caterpillars later turn into butterflies.

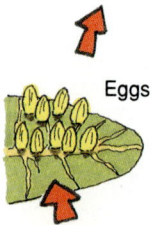

The Large White butterfly

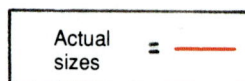

Actual sizes = —

BEAN SEED GRUBS

The adult is a fly which lays eggs in soil. Grubs hatch out and eat pea and bean seeds.

CABBAGE ROOT MAGGOTS

The adult is a fly which lays eggs in soil. The maggot eats the roots of cabbages, broccoli, radishes and turnips.

FLEA BEETLES

These feed on the leaves of vegetables in the cabbage family.

RED SPIDER MITES

These usually attack fruit. But they don't mind eating courgettes for a change!

SLUGS

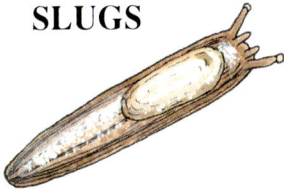

There are lots of different sorts of slugs. They usually like eating your plants at night or in damp weather. They often shelter out of sight in the day.

SNAILS

These are like slugs which carry their shelter with them. They eat plant leaves and shoots too. They like courgettes, as do slugs.

THRIPS

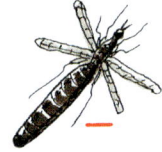

There are several sorts of these small insects. They often eat bean leaves or onions.

WHITEFLY

Lots of these may gather under the leaves of your crops. They suck the leaf sap from the veins.

COLORADO BEETLES

Watch out for these. They attack potato crops and can do a lot of damage. In some countries, you have to tell the police if you find one!

FACING FUNGUS FACTS

You may also have problems with fungi. There are thousands of different sorts of moulds, mildews, rots and rusts which can damage your plants.

WHAT TO DO...

1. Look out for powdery growths on your plants. Carefully pull off damaged leaves before the fungus spreads. Put them in a bag in the rubbish bin.

2. You can spray the healthy leaves with an organic seaweed spray. This will slow down or stop the spread of fungi. Get a bottle of seaweed spray from a garden centre. Or you could make your own if you live near the sea...

3. Next year, remember not to plant the same crops in the same spot. Why? - (see page 30).

Collect some seaweed...

Soak it in water for a few days...

Spray the liquid on your plants...

If you've got a small plot, you probably won't get many pests. And if you do, other animals will come and eat them! So you should try to

MAKE YOUR FRIENDS WELCOME!...

Snail for tea chicks!

Squawk!

Erk!

BIRDS

Many birds eat grubs, maggots, snails and flies. You can attract these birds by making nesting boxes for them.

ANTHOCORIDS

These insects eat mites, caterpillars and weevils. They like to live in untidy vegetation.

GROUND BEETLES

ROVE BEETLES

These eat maggots, weevils, slugs and grubs. They love to hide in a mulch of bark chips. Don't cut your lawn short. They like to live in long grass too.

FROGS

These eat lots of caterpillars, slugs and insects. Why not build a small pond for frogs?

HOVERFLY LARVAE

These can eat an aphid a minute! The adults live on nectar from some wild flowers.

LADYBIRDS AND LARVAE

These love eating aphids. They like a hedge to sleep in during winter.

Here's how to borrow ladybirds from a neighbour...

Find a shrub with some ladybirds on it. Hold an umbrella upside down underneath it. Shake the shrub gently. Take the umbrella back to your plot. Open the umbrella above your plants!

PARASITIC WASPS

The adults eat nectar and pollen. They lay their eggs inside aphids. The young eat the aphids' insides.

LACEWINGS AND LARVAE

These like eating aphids too. The adults also need flower pollen.

TOADS

Croak!

These eat insects, slugs and maggots. Make a toad box. It will encourage a toad to live in your garden!

MORE SPRAYS...

Sometimes, aphids, slugs and maggots move in too quickly for your friends to deal with. Or there may be too many of them for your friends to eat! Then you may need to use some organic sprays...

Come on lazybones ladybirds! Wake up and keep on eating!

Zzzzzz!

Phew! I'm full!

CHOMP!

1. GARLIC

Soak some crushed garlic in water for a day. Spray the liquid on your plants. This will discourage slugs but won't hurt other animals.

2. SOFT SOAP

Make a spray from soft soap. It will stop aphids but won't hurt ladybirds or lacewings.

SOFT SOAP

But... don't overdo the spraying. Remember, your little friends need something to eat. If you kill all their food, they may starve and die too!..

I'm starving! I can't find any aphids anywhere!

Me neither!

I think I'll pull up this dandelion!

Eek! What's happening?

Aargh! I think we're being weeded!

Some of your adult insect friends don't feed on pests. They feed on nearby plants instead. So don't just pull weeds from your plot. Some of your friends may be living on them.

While you're at the garden centre, think about getting a bin for

YOUR COMPOST HEAP!

WHAT'S COMPOST FOR?

Chemical particles in soil

This year...

Next year...

1. Vegetable roots take water and soil chemicals from the soil. These make the plant grow (see page 2).

2. Your vegetables turn the chemicals into plant material. You pick and eat the plants.

3. Now there are fewer soil chemicals left in the soil. Next year's crops will be smaller and fewer.

Autumn

Spring

Where will we get some dead vegetation from?

Dunno!

Let's look next door!

Hah!

4. In the wild, vegetation dies down after summer. It rots in the soil. This returns the soil chemicals to the soil. Then new plants can grow.

5. So you need to feed dead vegetation back in to the soil of your plot too. This will feed next year's crops.

6. A compost heap is a pile of dead vegetation. It rots down and turns back into useful soil chemicals.

You could buy a bag of compost every year. Or you could buy a compost bin and make your own. Fill up your bin with soft, dead vegetation. Follow the maker's instructions.

Vegetable peelings and leaves

Dinner scraps (no meat)

Hedge trimmings

Some grass cuttings

£59·95

24

BUT... you could save on the cost of a compost bin too!
In summer, get an adult to help you...

MAKE YOUR OWN COMPOST HEAP!

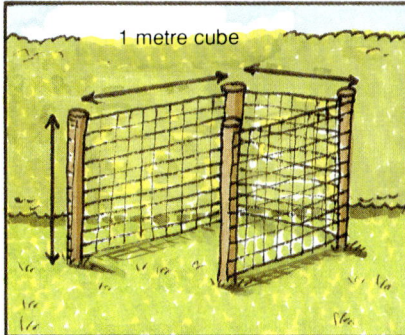

1 metre cube

1. Hammer four thick stakes into the ground. Nail wire mesh round three sides.

2. Put some tree branches inside. This lets the air in underneath.

3. Load up with your dead vegetation. Nail wire mesh on the front.

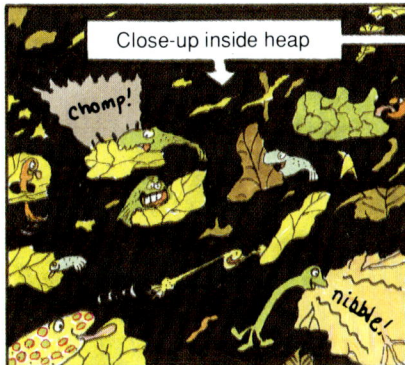

Close-up inside heap

chomp!

nibble!

4. Bacteria will soon start breaking down the vegetable matter.

Phew! It's too hot now!

It's just right for us though!

5. The heap will heat up. Heat-loving bacteria and fungi will arrive.

6. Keep the heap damp, but not too wet. If it rains a lot, put a bit of old carpet on top.

7. Turn the heap over with a garden fork about twice a month. Then all parts of the heap will get a chance to rot.

POO!

NIFF

PHOOR!

8. Your heap may not work at first. It may get slimy and smelly. If so, break it up and start again.

It smells lovely now!

Mmm!

9. The compost should be ready after about four months. Dig it into your plot in autumn or spring (see page 17).

Perhaps you don't have a garden.
Or you can't get a plot of soil.
Maybe you're just plain lazy?..

Never mind, you can still have

A MINI-FARM IN YOUR BEDROOM!

The Adventures of Lazy Person...

THE END

A TOMATO SOURCE...

You can buy a complete tomato-growing kit from garden centres and some supermarkets. All you need to do is follow the instructions on the box. Wake up to a tomato breakfast!..

TOMATO KIT

EEK!

BILLY'S BED

MUSHROOM KIT

A MUSHROOM BED...

Why not make room for mushrooms? Mushrooms can be bought as a kit too. They don't need much light, so you can grow them under your bed. Watch out though. They may grow faster and bigger than you think!..

28

MUNG BEANS AMONG YOUR JEANS...

You've probably grown mustard and cress at school. Why not try growing bean sprouts like the ones from a chinese takeaway?..
(You can grow fenugreek, alfalfa and chick peas like this too!)

1. Get a packet of dried mung beans. They're sometimes called moong beans. Soak a handful of them in clean water for a day.

2. Put a clean paper kitchen cloth in a flat bowl. Drop in the beans. Dampen the cloth.

3. Put the bowl in a warm, dark place. A clothes cupboard will do. Keep the beans moist with water from your sprayer.

4. After about four days, the bean sprouts will have grown as long as your little finger. Put them in a cheese sandwich – yummy!

PLANT A PLANT-POT POTATO PLANT...

1. Leave a few potatoes in a dark place. If you're lucky, white shoots will grow from them.

2. Put each potato into a big plant-pot of damp soil. Don't break any of the shoots.

3. Put the pots on a windowsill. Keep the soil damp, and the potatoes covered by the soil. A green plant will grow in each pot. Flowers will appear after a few weeks.

4. After the flowers have died, empty the plant-pots. Count your potato crop. Then wash, boil and eat them with butter – lovely!

Soon it will be # HARVEST-TIME in your plot.

- Make sure you pick your sunflower seeds before the birds spot them.

- Pick your beans, broccoli and courgettes as they become ripe.

- Some root vegetables can be left in the soil. Harvest them as you need them. Read your seed packets for information on these.

- Remember to keep notes of where each crop was grown.

AND NEXT YEAR...

Remember rotation (page 5)? You'll need to rotate your crops too. This helps to keep the soil fertile. And it stops pests and fungi from building up. Here's a complicated rotation suggestion for your plot for the next three years...

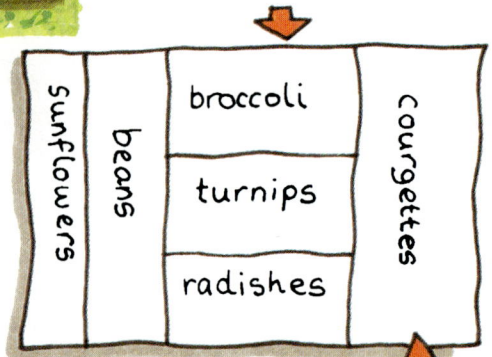

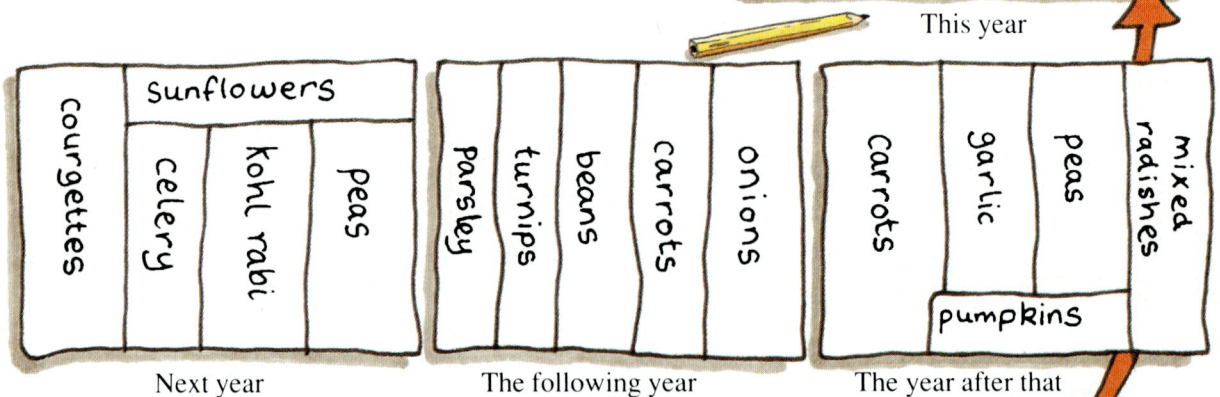

sunflowers	beans	broccoli	courgettes
		turnips	
		radishes	

This year

| courgettes | sunflowers | | | |
| | celery | kohl rabi | peas |

Next year

| parsley | turnips | beans | carrots | onions |

The following year

| carrots | garlic | peas | mixed radishes |
| | | pumpkins | |

The year after that

...And then you can go back to this year's plot plan!

EATING...

You might not have much to harvest. On the other hand, you might have too much to handle!

See if you can grow more difficult crops next year. Try celery, or kohl rabi. Grow peas instead of beans. Experiment!

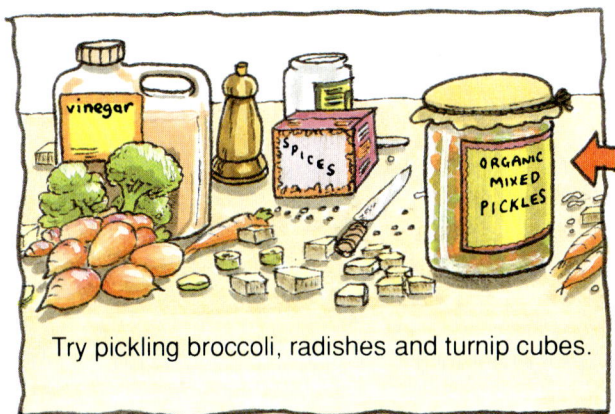

> Didn't we do well!

> And all from just a few seeds!

> We'll have to open a shop!

Try pickling broccoli, radishes and turnip cubes.

If you've got too many vegetables to eat, try pickling them. It's easy to do. BUT... there isn't enough space in this book to tell you all about it. Ask your parents, or get a book about pickling from the library.

You can make a great salad out of the six vegetables on pages 14 and 15. But the courgettes, chopped turnips and broccoli taste better lightly cooked. Get an adult to help you to prepare them. And get your parents to help you to eat them!..

> Eat your greens Mom. They're good for you!

> Tasty too!

> There's plenty more!

FREE FOOD

OR... you could give them away! Then your friends and neighbours will find out how delicious organic vegetables are. It may encourage them to become organic gardeners themselves!..

Pretty soon your neighbourhood could look like an organic farm!..

LOOK AFTER THE SOIL...
AND THE SOIL WILL
LOOK AFTER YOU!

INDEX